How to Buy, Fix and Sell Your Property and Make a Ton of Money

ERNIE BRAVEBOY

CONTENTS

Get Your Free Copy of

How to be a Real Estate Millionaire

To Get Your Free Copy, Open the Link

https://ebraveboy_3ee2.gr8.com/

Introduction

I want to thank you and congratulate you for buying the book, *"How to Buy, Fix and Sell Your Property and Make a Ton of Money"*.

This book has lots of actionable information on how to buy, fix and sell property and make tons of money.

One question many of us ask is, "Can I reach a comfortable level of financial freedom and be able to retire comfortably when my time to retire comes?" Perhaps even more importantly, while most of us are often sure about the importance of investing for the future and retirement, very few of us are sure about what to invest in or where to invest.

If you seek financial stability and freedom, you probably have a ton of questions about how to go about it.

The current financial world is just as intimidating as it is intriguing. With that said, with proper insight, investing can be your most lucrative endeavor. In particular, real estate investing has consistently continued to prove that it can serve as a reliable source of income for any intelligent and prudent investor. I know that many would be real estate investors only think of investing in rental properties but the truth is that there is more to real estate investing than rental properties. More precisely, this book will focus mainly on real estate flipping i.e. buying, repairing then selling of properties at a massive profit. Many investors have flipped thousands of properties in all market conditions proving that indeed, real estate flipping is a very viable investment strategy and one of the best routes to financial freedom.

Unlike most beginner real estate flippers, you are very lucky because with this guide at hand, you have everything you need to prepare as you seek to become a wildly profitable real estate investor. In this book, we shall talk about how to analyze the different kinds of real estate investment options available, how to purchase them, the ins and outs of financing, fixing/renovating and selling (and so much more). We are going to exhume, investigate, and deeply interrogate everything you need to know to become a good real estate investor. Let's begin.

Thanks again for buying this book. I hope you enjoy it!

WHY SHOULD YOU VENTURE INTO

PROPERTY FLIPPING?

As I already stated, there is more to property investing than investing in rental property. You can instead pursue property investing as a flipper whereby you buy distressed property that you believe is being sold at a price that is far much lower than its market value, fix it up then put it up for sale. You buy the houses from foreclosure, auctions or bank short sales at a great discount. The question you might have is; so why should you pursue this investing option when you can simply rent out property and expect a regular cash flow in form of rent? Here are some reasons that will fuel your desire to go all out into flipping:

Why Should You Venture Into Property Flipping?

1. You Earn Quick Profits

Think of buying property for rent and compare it with buying it, repairing and then selling it off and you will realize that with real estate flipping, the returns on investment are fast. After selling, you already have your profit if you pursue the flipping route. But with investing in rental property, it will take several years or close to a decade before you can recoup your investment. This is definitely something that is attractive enough to make you want to pursue real estate flipping. Statistics have it that with flipping, you can earn returns that are much higher than the annual US median salary.

2. Gives You Experience on Different Aspects of Real Estate

Flipping entails every bit of real estate investing in the process of negotiating property before purchase, fixing it up (construction) and selling. Essentially, you get experience in construction, get to understand your local market, get to know how to estimate construction costs and many other aspects of real estate. Let me explain some of these:

✓ *You understand the local market if you are a flipper*

Flipping is very involving because before you settle for any given deal, you must do your research well. In this case, you browse through for sale ads, go round different neighborhoods looking for 'for sale' sign boards and talk to realtors in a given area. Through all this, you get to know the properties that are recently sold (how much they sold for, their condition, features etc.), and what's on sale in a bid to know the market well to know what's hot in a given area. And when you put up the property for sale, you get to know what buyers are looking for, their price points and much more that you can use to become a better flipper.

✓ *You get to learn various other aspects of real estate in general*

The flipping process will open your eyes to aspects of real estate investing that you otherwise would not know had you pursued another route to real estate investing. For instance, you get to know such things as the difference between buying foreclosed property and short sales.

✓ *You get to understand the intricacies of construction*

As a flipper, you will always be repairing, remodeling or

renovating the houses that you purchase before you sell them. This process can give you lots of great insight about construction, which you can use to make your houses better, cut costs and achieve different other goals. for instance, you get to know material costs, know about electrical repairs, plumbing and much more. As you do this, over time, you become a pro at spotting structural issues when purchasing property to flip and develop an understanding of potential dangers like asbestos and mold. All this will put you squarely on the path to success.

✓ *You get to learn how to anticipate costs like a pro*

The process of fixing up properties for sale will be an eye opening one. As you go along, you will be able to correctly anticipate various aspects of real estate flipping, which are critical if you want to excel. This will help you to budget for such things like delays in delay of materials, construction delays, holding costs, contractor disputes and much more.

3. Flipping will help you increase your network

The thing is, you cannot do flipping alone; you have to rely on many other players in the industry such as contractors, realtors, attorneys, insurance brokers, building inspectors and many others who will share different skills as you interact with them. These networks will prove useful in future.

4. Change of perspective

Ultimately, flipping will also be a great avenue for you to make lots of money and feel good about seeing value in properties that seem rundown. The process itself opens your perspective so that you can start seeing run down properties as the value they present.

Just as there are many benefits of real estate flipping, there are also some unsettling truths about real estate that you should appreciate if you really want to flip for the long haul.

Buyer Beware: Some Unsettling Truths about Flipping

While flipping is profitable, the unfortunate truth is that things don't go as they go on TV. In fact:

✓ *You could lose money instead of making a profit*

It is not uncommon for beginners to make costly mistakes especially in estimating how much it costs to fix the property and the prices they expect the properties to sell. These mistakes can be costly because they eat into your profit and make it hard for you to sell the property competitively. There are several factors that could easily eat into your profit: new materials that you had not budgeted for, permit delays, which ultimately end up making you to tie your money for longer than expected, contractor delays and other unexpected occurrences. Therefore, make sure you don't put all your eggs in one basket; commit money that you can afford to have tied for a while especially in the beginning.

✓ *Taxes can eat into your profits*

The city might decide to increase property taxes just when you've completed the renovations, something that might make it hard to find a buyer. Ultimately, you might be forced to shelf the tax burden and might even drive away buyers because of the higher tax bill.

This ultimately affects your holding costs:

✓ *Holding costs could be unsustainable*

You might not sell the property as fast as you might have envisioned. But this does not stop the mortgage repayments (assuming you got the property on mortgage) and insurance even when you are not making money. You might also be forced to do some additional repairs over time if the property doesn't sell as fast. These things can eat into your profits and tie your money such that you cannot do much.

✓ *A ready supply of money is critical*

With flipping, you cannot rely on money that you are uncertain about e.g. an unapproved mortgage, which we all know could be rejected. In this business model, money changes hands pretty fast so you will need a ready supply of money if you really want to close deals fast, fix property fast and make the most profits just as fast.

Time is of importance because the more time that passes, the more money you stand to lose due to taxes and various holding costs. This doesn't mean that you must have hundreds of thousands of dollars idling in the bank so that you can flip successfully. On the contrary, you can actually make money as a flipper without spending a lot of money. For instance, you can use borrowed funds (from a bank, hard money lenders, private money lenders, friend or whichever other place you can borrow from) or partner with someone who has money where you will be doing the leg work where you share 50/50.

We will discuss more on external financing in the last chapter.

Obviously, these are facts that you can mitigate by doing your homework pretty well. For instance, you can reduce your odds of making losses by estimating the selling after repair (ARV) as well as the cost of repair as accurately as you possibly can. As for taxes and holding costs, you can keep these costs low by ensuring that you sell the property as fast as you can by employing different marketing strategies while taking into consideration the fact that you've done your math well as far as pricing is concerned.

And for the supply of money, the best solution is to network; get out there and know people who can finance your venture. You can find potential financiers from some of the following places:

✓ Real estate investor meetings at Meetup.com
✓ Your local Real Estate Investors Association (REIA) meetings
✓ Local charities
✓ You can as well form your own local real estate investors association
✓ Your local chapter for Business Networking International
✓ Your Local Chamber Of Commerce

For you to get in, you shouldn't expect investors to find you; you go to them and pitch your idea to them.

So how exactly should you go about it? Let's start learning the intricacies of investing in real estate as a flipper.

Super Important NOTE

Before we discuss anything else pertaining flipping, you need to keep something in mind: *never ever purchase a real estate investment in your own name directly*. There are many reasons for this, some of which associate with protection of personal asset. For instance, if something goes wrong and you have to deal with something such as a lawsuit settlement exceeding your insurance coverage, both you as well as your advisors will require the capacity to place the entity that can hold the property during bankruptcy so that you will have an opportunity to leave and fight another day.

In this regard, you have several options at your disposal:

The Legal Entity Option

All experienced real estate investors will tell you that

they use a legal structure called Limited Liability Company (LLC) or Limited Partnership (LP). What do these mean?

LLC: An LLC is a form of business that combines the benefits of limited partnerships with those of a corporation. Its most prominent advantages include asset protection, pass-through taxation, less rigid management structures, and limited compliance rules.

All limited liability operating companies usually work within the confines of a contract that investors sign amongst themselves before forming the company. Also called an LLC operating agreement, this contract provides important information regarding the company's policies, procedures, and priorities. Many states require that investors present it alongside their application for incorporation.

Therefore, you have to consider talking to your accountant and attorney about doing the same as it can save you a myriad of financial hardships along the way: always hope for the best but plan for the worst.

Limited Partnership: A limited partnership is an entity whose organization allows for real estate investing. Typically, a real estate limited partnership is with an experienced real estate development firm that serves as the general partner, or property manager. Investors from outside are sought to finance the real estate project and in exchange, they get a share of ownership as limited partners.

You can think of limited partners as stockholders in a public company because they possess limited influence in the limited partnership's business operations. Nonetheless, limited partners also possess limited liability. If the real estate limited partnership loses, the limited partners are liable only for their capital contribution's amount.

You only require a few hundred dollars to set up these special legal structures—if you want a reputable attorney in a good-sized city, you will probably have to part with a few thousand dollars. The requirements for paperwork filing are not that overwhelming and you could use separate LLC for each of your real estate investments in a technique we call 'asset separation,' a technique that protects both you and your holdings. What this technique does is, in case one of the properties gets into any trouble, you could easily file for a bankruptcy for that property without anyone getting hurt (so long as you did not conversely sign an agreement like a promissory note that made your liabilities cross-collaterals).

Now that we have that understanding, let us now discuss how to get started as a real estate flipper.

HOW TO FLIP REAL ESTATE LIKE A PRO

It is true that home flipping is a profitable business model but let me make one thing clear; as a beginner, you might not make hundreds of thousands of dollars in a single sale. Nonetheless, with an average 35% return on investment, which equates to roughly $72,450 on the table, you can bet that even if you flip one property per year, you will still have enough money to take care of your bills at the end of the year. But keep in mind that flipping is not as easy as they make it look on TV where all you do is lowball on property that was previously unsalable, get lightning speed repair guys at work and you have potential buyers lining with loads of cash on your doorstep wanting the property. While it sounds easy in theory, it takes hard work to make that work. Here are some points that you must keep in mind:

Before we begin, we first have to make sure your financial house is in order:

Step 1: Consider Your Financial Ability versus the Potential Costs

Flipping is a capital intensive investment venture. Therefore, it is only logical that you have your finances in order as you get started. Before you begin, the first thing you need to ask yourself is; can your current finances handle this sort of commitment? Are you on course to achieve your retirement-saving goals? Just in case you are wondering, real estate investing should never be a replacement for retirement savings. If you have a personal financial planner, does he/she back your decision to direct your money into this sort of investment?

Can you afford it? How much are you willing to spend on the properties that you are going to be flipping? Studies have shown that houses that flip best are those priced between $100,000 and $300,000 so before you do anything, determine whether you can afford this kind of financial commitment and then decide how much you are willing to spend on the property. This will be important in future, as it will help you to narrow down on the properties that you could flip.

After carefully considering your total financial picture, you can now map out the costs up front. One thing you will have to do is factor in the down payment and the estimated monthly mortgage bill if you opt for external financing. You also need to take some time to calculate every expense that may come your way including new appliances, paint or a new roof, and other expenses. You also want to plan to set aside some money for maintenance and repairs. There is no exact money here as it all varies from property to property. Nonetheless, many real estate consultants have started suggesting a budgeting of between $100-$200 each month for a single family home or 10-15%

of multi-family's property rent.

Also, take a look at this public service announcement: *"if you are considering covering some of these costs by tapping into your 401(k) (the employer-sponsored retirement savings plan), you should rethink that option. The reason is that by doing so, you will fail to gain from the benefits of compound growth and there is a chance that you will be sacrificing your future retirement fund."*

Lastly, ask yourself this question; what if you lose your source of income? Ensure you put into consideration how you will deal with any changes in your financial situation. Before you do anything, you will need to be careful not to overstretch yourself with financial commitments that you cannot handle. Remember that your savings should be able to cover the deposit, expenses such as mortgage fees, repair costs and everything in between. This is important because supply of money is critical if you want to flip the property fast enough so as to maximize profits.

Step 2: Assemble Your Flipping Team

When you have the issue of financing sorted, now you can start building the team that will take you through the flipping process. You cannot do everything alone, whether you are a beginner or an expert flipper.

What's the role of this 'team', you might ask? Well, the team will help you in every step of the way to ensure you move the process as swiftly as possible without making any avoidable mistakes. For instance, your team will need to comprise of people who will help you to find properties that you can flip, people who will help you to objectively estimate the cost of repairs and a team that will help you throughout the selling process. As a beginner, the collective wisdom of everyone on the team will undoubtedly enable you to make huge strides in flipping successfully and without making losses. You can think of this team as a 'mastermind' group, which will help you to focus, be more productive and avoid making dump mistakes along the way. So in essence, your team should be made of professionals such as money lenders, accountants, insurance specialists, architects, contractors and real estate brokers. The input from these professionals will undoubtedly help shorten your learning curve while ensuring that you start making money from flipping houses from the very first house that you flip. After successfully flipping several houses, you should perhaps be in a position to reduce your reliance on proccessionals so that you can do it all by yourself. This will ultimately enable you to learn more as you do stuff on your own.

Note: Some people will argue that you should start on your own and learn the ropes as you go along, as using a team of professionals makes you overly dependent on them. Well, I believe this is the wrong route to take. Think about it; with this approach, you are likely to have a hard time finding property to flip, are likely to pay too much to acquire the property and are subsequently likely to overestimate or underestimate repair costs. You don't want that to happen because either way, you make your flipping process harder than necessary. In fact, you might even end up giving up flipping altogether if you make losses after flipping or find it is just too much work.

Note: Also, as you assemble your team, make sure to get the necessary tools that will make the process easy for you. For instance, you will need to go out to different stores that sell construction materials to help you get prices of the different materials, which you will need to fix the property. Use this pre-prepared form to record everything. When that time comes when you need to check for the prices of different items, insist on checking these prices in stores that are as near to the property as possible. This will help you to keep the costs low.

Once you have the people and tools that you need, now you can start looking for houses to flip.

Step 3: Look For a House to Flip

The truth is; finding flip-worthy houses is a challenge for many people. Just because a property is on sale doesn't mean it is good for flipping. This is where you start using your flipping team (real estate agents as well as wholesalers) that you assembled above to help you with the process. As a beginner, you should find a house that doesn't require a lot of repair work especially to make the process easy for you. The ideal scenario is to buy the house for a fairly low price, supervise the process of rehab very quickly and cheaply and then sell it. From then on, you can continue increasing your appetite for properties that require lots of repair work.

Here are some great ideas on how to find houses to flip:
✓ MLS (Multiple Listing Service): If you are not a realtor, it is best to use the services of your realtor to find properties to flip on MLS.
✓ Join a real estate investment group then share information
✓ Through your networks; you never know; A flipper who perhaps doesn't have enough financing to take care of several flips at the same time (after having his/her bids accepted) might perhaps want to pass the deal to you to ensure he does not ruin his/her reputation as someone who doesn't honor his/her accepted bids.
✓ Estate and foreclosure auctions: This is great especially if you have cold hard cash.

✓ Classifieds
✓ Align yourself to wholesalers; they will undoubtedly push deals to you so that you can focus on repairs and selling
✓ Your flipping team; they will undoubtedly push a deal or two to you
✓ A real estate who specializes in REO (real estate owned by lender because of defaulted payment)
✓ Drive around the neighborhood that you want to buy property in; you might find something!

With all these avenues for finding properties that you can flip, you should undoubtedly have an easy time in getting something.

As you look for properties to flip, you need to keep in mind some important points:

1: Location is King

The law of demand and supply here reins. This is largely dependent on the location; you need a market that has an ample supply of homes that you can actually buy low as well as a good number of buyers who you can sell high to. In this case, ideal markets for flippers are those market that not only have a huge number of affordable properties that are distressed but a significantly high demand for recently renovated properties. This is very important because if this balance does not exist, you are likely to have a hard time selling a flipped home. Some of the best markets for flippers include Central Florida, Chicago, Memphis, Pittsburg, Tucson, Detroit and Baltimore. Markets where buyers are looking for brand new houses and the available affordable houses are few are not good for flippers. So you shouldn't really expect to thrive as a flipper on markets like Houston, Phoenix, Las Vegas and San Francisco unless you are willing to accept a low profit margin as well as a longer period before you close a deal.

Tip: Proximity

In the weeks and possibly months to come, you will work on this property. Are you committed to working all day and then driving an hour to get home? It is not always affordable to invest in a house that is too far from your residence since if you do, you will spend more money on fuel, use more time, and ultimately take longer to fix up the house.

As you consider the location, you should also make sure that you are offering what customers in each market are looking for.

2: Remember that the customer is the king so meet his/her needs

Whichever market that you settle for, make sure to research to find what houses are selling and the prices at which they are selling. You don't want to be selling condos when everyone in the area is looking for 3 bedroom homes for instance. As you do this, keep in mind that the price range for flipped houses ranges between $100,000 and $300,000 with $100,000-300,000 having the highest profits. Also, keep in mind that low priced homes don't attract really a significant profit, as the costs might actually be depleted by the repair costs. You could lose up to $2% for homes that are priced between $50,000 and below.

But even as you look for homes to flip, make sure that you aim to flip homes that require the least amount of work to get them to a sellable state.

3: Aim for homes that require the least amount of work

I know you might think that the more rundown a house is, the more you can negotiate the price down. But be careful with this thinking; repair costs can easily escalate to amounts that only make you to break even. Other than losing money, the process of fixing such homes is hectic and frustrating because you are even likely to see new areas that require repairs that you never even noticed before. To avoid all that, go for homes that require the nothing more than cosmetic changes or something close to that to prepare them for sale. For instance, you can give the home a fresh coat of paint, replace some broken windows, install a new carpet, perform some inexpensive yard work, refine the kitchen cabinets, add some shiny hardware, etc. But if you have to replace all the duct work or the roof, it is best that you pass the deal because you just cannot estimate with certainty (especially as a beginner) how much the costs might end up being.

As you go around checking for houses to flip, you will undoubtedly need to give an offer to the sellers. So how exactly do you do it to ensure you don't end up giving a very low offer that ends up being rejected and perhaps beaten by competitors or one that is too high such that you end up eating into your profits? Here is a general rule you should observe while giving offers:

Step 4: Use The 70% Rule to Determine Your Maximum Offer

Before you make an offer, ask yourself this question; "how much will this home sell after I have repaired it?" Obviously, don't just answer the question without backing it up with research. Do a market research of comparative homes in the neighborhood that have been flipped in the last 90 days to come up with an estimate of just how much the current property might sell for. Although you can have a realtor do the calculations for you, I would still recommend that you learn how to do these simple calculations, as this will start weaning you off your reliance on professionals. To get started, you need to check sites such as Zillow.com, Trulia.com, Movoto.com and

Realtor.com to determine the comparative houses that have sold in the area in the recent past. Make sure to also ask around; ask your real estate agent and other industry players in the area to know how much different houses have sold for. You ought to get through MLS (Multiple Listing Service) to get comparative houses that have been flipped recently. As you do the research, make sure to consider the following:

✓ Consider houses that have actually been sold and not those that are still on sale

✓ Make sure to check the floor area (square footage) where necessary; you want to compare houses that are as close to similar as possible. But if you don't find any property that is of the same square footage as the one on sale and with similar amenities, you can divide the sales price by the square footage to get the price per square foot then multiply the figure you get by the square area of the house you want to flip by the figure you got above. Assuming all factors are held constant, you should have a pretty reliable figure.

✓ The more recent, the better: Insist on comparing houses that have been sold within the last 90 days. Do not exceed 90 days.

✓ And if you cannot find any comparable properties that have been sold in the last 90 days, that's a red flag; it means that the properties here are not in high demand or the prices are inflated.

✓ Bathrooms and bedrooms do make a difference in pricing properties. As such, make sure to adjust the price accordingly if you cannot find a house that has the exact bedrooms and bathrooms.

✓ As you compare, keep in mind that some features like the newness of the kitchen, type of roof, the bathrooms or heating systems can affect the price of the property so ensure to adjust upwards or downwards depending on whether the property you want to flip has or does not have in respect to a comparative house sold in the last 90 days.

These are things that your realtor can do for you but as I have mentioned, you also want to be aware of what is happening, as you will need that understanding for future flips.

Once you have the estimated price of the property after flipping it, multiply it by 70% then subtract the total estimated cost of repairs from the resulting figure. Here is an example; assume that you think you can sell a house for $140,000 after spending $20,000 to fix it. Your offer should be something like this:

140,000x70%=98,000

98,000-20,000=78,000

This essentially means the most you should offer for the property is $78,000 to ensure you make an acceptable profit.

This brings something very important into the picture i.e. the repair costs. So how exactly do you come up with a figure that is as close to the actual cost of repair as possible? Before you come up with a figure for the repair costs, you need to do your ground work to ensure you don't underestimate the costs only for you to end up making losses or overestimate repair costs only for you end up giving a low offer, which will only make the seller unwilling to sell the property to you. Let's discuss how to come up with a figure for the estimated cost of repairs.

Step 5: Estimate the Cost of Repairs

Before you commit your money by giving an offer, the seller ought to agree that you do an inspection just so you know how much you might perhaps spend to fix the house.

The more thorough the inspection is, the higher the chances that you will have very accurate estimates.

We can categorize the cost of repairs into 3 broad types of costs namely the material costs, labor costs and overall costs. You need to use different approaches to estimate different costs.

For instance, for material costs, you can estimate these correctly by simply spending visiting your local home improvement stores e.g. Lowe's Home Improvement, for specific rooms in a house so that you know how much various items cost. This approach of estimating the cost of repairing one room at a time will make it easier for you to come up with an objective figure. To execute the process, simply divide a house into different sections/room categories. For instance, you can have such categories/sections as paint, flooring, kitchen, landscaping, stucco, kitchen, plumbing fixtures, window/sliders, electrical fixtures, roof, door, garage, foundation, interior doors etc. Once you have the categories, you can now start narrowing down your search for the price of materials for repairing each room. This will make it easy for you to do quick calculations especially when you get used to the calculations. For instance, with practice, you can estimate the cost of replacing showerheads, glass door enclosure, vanity, sink, mirror, new toilet and gut to about $2500 per bathroom, which means that if you walk in and out of a bathroom, you can do quick calculations to determine an estimated amount. As such, as you go around the house when checking out the house, you can simply add the constituent cost categories as you go along. The more you know about the cost of materials, the easier it is going to be for you to get figures that are as close to the correct figure as possible. As you go about checking a house that is on sale, make sure to bring your notebook with you to write down the price range for materials such as fixtures, vanities, blinds, paint, laminate, tile, carpet as well as ceiling fans. It is best to prepare a spreadsheet so that you can easily note down each of the items for easy tabulation.

As for labor costs, the best place to know the actual costs is to ask contractors and other investors to know how much labor costs (you can also use the RSMeans Cost Calculator or the National Repair & Modeling Estimator). This makes it critical to network with the local service providers, as this will be a good avenue to find out about the local labor charges. You also want to use referrals to ensure the people you get people who are dependable and affordable.

After doing that, come up with price a range for different cost items. For example, you can estimate the cost of new light fixtures for a 1500 square foot house to range between $500 and $1000 depending on their quality, the number of units that are needed, the charges for different technicians, the value of the neighborhood as well as your ability to find specific materials on sale. Divide the sum of the lower amount and the upper amount by two to get an estimated average cost for that particular cost item.

While you can always get these cost estimates from a contractor, it is recommended that you compare quotes from several contractors to get a feel of the market. Obviously, don't just choose the cheapest; he/she might cost you money in the long term.

As you flip, keep in mind that the different cost estimates that you have are not fixed; some are likely to vary depending on different factors. For instance, you might have estimated that you need to do a replacement of the air conditioning system (which costs about $3000-4000) only for you to finally discover that a simple repair of less than $300 is sufficient to restore its functioning. When you have your estimates for each category of items, simply get the totals and follow the math we discussed earlier to determine how much you should pay for the property in question.

Once you have the estimates ready, the next step you should take is to get to work.

Tip: I would recommend that you have all the materials that you need ready even before you close the deal. The reason for this is to reduce time wasted in trying to get these things when your offer has already been accepted, as this wastes time. Before you purchase these items, have the seller agree that you can return the purchased items within a certain time window. With this approach, you will be sure that you will get a head start on rehabbing since you will have all you need to start the process of fixing the house immediately. When you have everything set, no unexpected turn of events can stop you from being on schedule. Ultimately, you will be able to manage costs such as utilities, taxes, maintenance, insurance etc. efficiently and realize profits very fast.

Power tip:

If you are going to deal with your flipping team, it is important that you written agreements on the charges for different services. You don't want to look as if you are using free services from your contractors, realtors, real estate agents and other service providers that are on your team. This is the stage where you want to come up with a budget that estimates the cost of repairs, holding costs, financing costs, carrying costs (utilities like gas, water and electricity, property tax, insurance, and condo fees), the cost of paying different professionals for services (e.g. realtor's fees, contractor's fees, legal fees, etc.) and other fees that will be incurred throughout the flipping process. Budgeting is critical, as it will help you to keep your costs in check. Moreover, by setting the budget, you can objectively state how much you are likely to spend on the flip as well as the possible profit margin. After the actual costs have been incurred, you will then be able to go back to the drawing board to determine the differences. The more flipping budgets that you prepare, the more you can compare them with the actual amount spent so that you can determine the margin of error and subsequently allocate an amount for the unexpected costs. In the end, you become a better flipper.

Part of the agreement should also state the scope of work with each member of your team as well as a time estimate on how long different activities will take before they are completed.

After estimating how much you should pay for the property, your next step is to give an offer to the seller who will then make a decision on whether your offer is attractive enough or not. As a rule of thumb, if you are bidding in an auction, never bid on something you've not seen; the property might be too run down, which is not a good place to start if you are a beginner.

Once you have a deal, it is time to use your attorney to get all the paperwork done i.e. a contract that clearly outlines all the terms. After you have the necessary papers ready and have paid the necessary amounts (down payment), you can now start working on your newly acquired property.

Step 6: Get the Repair Work Done Fast

The shorter the period you take to take care of repairs, the higher the likelihood that you will maximize profits. Moreover, the longer you have your capital tied up in the property, this means that you will have less of it available to finance other investments.

Essentially, you should aim to fix the property within 90 days but aiming for 150 days is also not too bad. Keep in mind that fixing up the property in less than 90 days doesn't mean you will sell it as fast (although it increases your odds of selling it fast); FHA won't allow mortgages for properties, which a seller has not held for more than 90 days. Moreover, Freddie Mac and Fannie Mae won't let anyone to resell property that they've bought through them for more than 20% of the purchase price within a 90 day period.

Keep in mind that you will need to oversee the process to get everything done to your specifications. Therefore, although you can rely on professionals to get the real job done, your presence is also important, as you will actually be able to fix the property in a way that you want if you are present. Moreover, being there will enable you to start estimating just how much it takes to complete different tasks in the repair process. This is very critical in estimating labor costs objectively.

Note:

You will need permits before you begin remodeling. By having the wrong permits, or displaying permits wrongly, you can welcome serious delays and perhaps fines from city inspectors. Therefore, as soon as the sale is final, apply for permits immediately. This will also help you create a timeline for projects, and with the associated deadlines, and help with the budget listed for every project. Ultimately, you and your contractors will be in a better position to get the renovations done quickly and remain within budget if you don't have unexpected delays to worry about.

Note that when you do your estimations on the cost of any job, experts will advise you to add 20% to the last estimate. The reason is that it is always going to cost you more than you think, always.

Step 6: Put the House on Sale

Once the house is ready, it is time to sell it. You definitely will need to price the house competitively while using the ARV as the benchmark.

As you are well aware, the faster you sell it, the more you will be able to keep such costs as carrying costs within budget. Therefore, make sure to use the services of everyone you can use to market the property to buyers.

Your team (realtors/real estate agents) will come in handy in ensuring that you put the house out there for the world to see. Nonetheless, this does not mean that you cannot market the property by yourself.

You can list it on:

✓ **Different Property Marketplaces**

MLS: You will need a registered realtor who has an active MLS membership to list the property.

Zillow.com

Realtor.com

Redfin.com

Loopnet.com

✓ **Put up a for sale sign board**

✓ Use the networks that you have been building to get word out that you have a house for sale

✓ Social media

✓ Newspaper ads

✓ Flyers

✓ Hosting an open day

Important: Marketing Tips!

Apart from the above marketing techniques, some other methods are quite different and very effective. To learn about these, keep reading.

Live Facebook events

Today, people love bragging about their life events on Facebook and tend to broadcast them to everyone as soon as they happen. If you sign up as an advertiser on Facebook, you gain access to, and can target these events within the geographical area that you are targeting.

For instance, you can target a campaign towards young couples below 35 years who have probably just moved to the city. If you specialized in new family-starter level homes, you can go with engagements, pregnancy, and marriages announcement. Definitely, you can have various ads show to the various life events–have one set of ads for baby announcements and another for marriages or engagements.

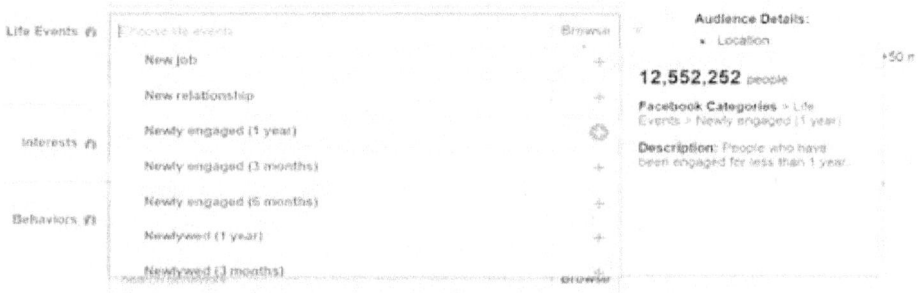

For more information about the audiences you can target when setting up your Facebook ad's targeting, check out this page.

Create a video footage of the space

Remote homebuyers looking to set up viewings before getting to town can be good targets with high quality video footages of your space.

Good videos usually showcase a space in a way the best pictures cannot. Therefore, you have to create a videos showing you (or someone else) going through the property, fitting in the space and enjoying every bit of it. With that, someone imagines him or herself living out his or her life in that exact space, which gets the potential buyer emotionally attached to it, thus making it more likely that the buyer will want to get in touch with you to come see the property firsthand.

Post the video on your website, social media pages, YouTube channel or any other relevant platform.

Sell the neighborhood

When approaching a property with the prospective buyer, you have to take enough time to point out all the perks of living in the neighborhood which can lead up to the actual location of the property which you know the buyer shall be interested in.

If you think the buyers are foodies, point out all the great restaurants and their delicious food items. If you think your buyers like a good nightlife, highlight the grand clubs and bars around. If art is what is important to the buyer, talk to them about the nearby art studios, music venues, and galleries.

By doing so, you will place the buyer in an imaginative state where he or she will start seeing him or herself living in, and enjoying the neighborhood before even seeing the property.

If the property is a bit less special, or is not something truly stellar, they will easily overlook more of its reservations than you would imagine especially if they have already developed an emotional attachment to the neighborhood.

Just to be clear, this is not about tricking your prospective buyers into a space they will not be happy with, or that which cannot work for them; it is about giving buyers something that is well functional and offers them the kind of life they are after.

Note: Stage the House for Sale

Buyers are really funny people. Something that seems seemingly unimportant to you and that might cost you less than $1000 to get done can make the difference between a deal or no deal. For instance, lawns that are not properly fixed, potholes on the driveway, some streaks of paint or an unclean house can make potential buyers to turn down the deal. Here is why: when people are buying houses, they don't their first order of business to be fixing different things around the house because you didn't do them well. The typical buyer wants to imagine him/herself living in the space when they step in the compound. Anything that the buyer imagines should ideally be about putting his/her touches to personalize the space. For instance, if you clean the house well, the buyer will perhaps be thinking how he/she will organize the stuff he/she has in the new space. You don't want to disrupt the buyer's thoughts by having construction materials still lying around the house. If need be, you can have lights affixed and various other fixtures affixed to make the space to feel warm and ready for occupation.

After finding a buyer, everything else is really about paperwork. Make sure to involve your attorney and accountant to help you determine how much tax you will need to pay. The experience from the members of your team will come in handy at this time, as they are likely to let you know what you should/should not do at this stage.

Once the deal is closed and all paperwork is done, all you need to do is to revisit the entire process, find which mistakes you made and learn from them so that you can use the knowledge to make better decisions in the next flip. Happy flipping!

If you don't have the money to finance a flip or feel it is too much work, you can instead opt to become a wholesaler. Let's learn how to go about it next.

WHOLESALING REAL ESTATE

In its simplest terms, wholesaling refers to the process of discovering great deals in real estate, writing a contract to get the deal, and then selling it to another buyer. Technically, the wholesaler does not actually own a piece of property he or she is selling at any given time.

He or she simply finds a great deal using various marketing strategies and places them under contract then sells the contract to another person for some 'assignment fee'. On average, this fee is usually between $500 and $5,000 or even more depending on the quality of the deal. The wholesaler is therefore some kind of an intermediary who earns revenue from finding deals.

While some wholesalers will sell their contracts to retail buyers, most of them choose to sell them to investors (such as house flippers) who in this case are the 'cash buyers'. In this case, the wholesaler can receive the agreed upon fee within weeks or even days and can create strong connections in the real estate fraternity.

With that said, you could begin with wholesaling because it has a reputation as being a simple strategy and one that carries low start-up costs. Since you don't have to own any property, there are no loan fees, rehab costs, banks, contractors, or other similar forms of 'complications'. This is why wholesaling is the most popular strategy taught by gurus in the real estate and one that often gets the most attention in the end.

As a wholesaler, you will engage in the process of continually looking for the best deals so that you have inventory to sell to other people. You should also have an ingenious marketing funnel that continually attracts leads. You must also constantly seek out buyers for the deals you acquire.

Perhaps the strongest quality of this strategy is that this strategy is one anyone can handle. Even if you have no money at all, you can do it because you do not necessarily require financial resources to construct your marketing funnel (but you really have to be very good at marketing). This is why the most people who are successful at implementing this strategy and have found themselves a good source of income are typically the ones who have managed to persist in building their skills of wholesaling while growing their knowledge of other profitable strategies.

How Wholesaling Works

If you are not sure where to begin as a wholesaler, follow this simple process:
1. Find property: This is as easy as finding any property on sale (on the MLS, direct mail, newspapers etc.)
2. Determine how much you ought to offer.

Although this works in a manner that is pretty similar to flipping, you have to factor the fact that you are selling the contract to flippers who have their ARV set and the maximum amount that they are willing to pay.

It makes sense that since your work is to find deals for other people, we begin at the end and work backwards. Assuming you are selling the property to a flipper, the flipper has to make money in the process too. The amount the end buyer will end up paying is called the ***maximum allowable offer (MAO).***

To find the MAO, let us start with the after repair value (ARV). The ARV is the final price the flipper is going to sell the property for.

Deduct out all the costs associated with the deal from this number; these costs include:

- The profit of the flipper
- The repair costs
- The fixed costs; this is how much the flipper will pay including holding and transaction costs (on both deals)
- Your profit as the wholesaler

If you would rather see the formula, it looks something like this:

MAO = (ARV) – (Profit of the flipper) – [Fixed Costs] – [Repair Costs] – [Wholesale Fee]

Let us look at an example:

You do your homework on a property and discover that the ARV can be $110,000. You also know that the average profit a flipper plans to make on such a property is $20,000.

After further research, you discover that the fixed costs on a flip are roughly $15,000, which includes the holding costs, then the realtor fees when the flipper sells it and finally the closing costs from start to end.

You also deduce that the building needs about $30,000 for material and labor to fix it up. Let's assume that you set your wholesaler fee at $5,000.

Thus:

MAO = (ARV) \$110,000 − (Flipper's profit) \$20,000 − (fixed costs) \$30,000 − (repair costs) 15,000 − (wholesale fee) \$5,000.

Maximum Allowable Offer = \$40,000.

The last thing we will discuss financing.

REAL ESTATE EXTERNAL FINANCING

We all know that how you finance any business operation can actually be the difference between dominance and failure.

Let us look at some of the best sources of capital you can consider in brief.

Note: Many of these will be most effective if you have mastered the art of flipping. You don't want to gamble with people's money when you are still starting out.

SBA 7 (A) Loans

SBA 7 (A) is specific for commercial Real Estate. This type of loan is essentially a mortgage supported by the United States Small Business Administration. These are some of the most common form of SBA loans and can help you buy or re-finance your commercial properties up to five million dollars. Of all the SBA 7(a) loans issued in 2016, 65 percent went to existing businesses and 35 percent went to new businesses.

This kind of loan will finance between 85% and 90% of the value of a commercial property, and as mentioned earlier, the Small Business Association guarantees a maximum loan of $5,000,000. Therefore, if you are going for this route, expect to take care of 10% and 15% of the purchase price. Nonetheless, as a well-qualified buyer, you can still have your cash down payment waived.

You can obtain the SBA 7 (a) loans through any lender approved by SBA. These lenders range from the smaller credit unions to the large traditional banks and private lenders. If you have a prior relationship with a credit union or bank, its more prudent to check with them first to see whether they are permitted to make the SBA loans, and whether they are PLP lenders.

A company such as SmartBiz shall help you get an SBA 7(a) for your commercial real estate faster than the old-school lenders. Therefore, be sure to check it out.

Traditional Commercial Mortgage

This is the standard commercial loan issued by a lending institution or a bank not backed by the federal government. You can use the traditional commercial mortgages to buy or refinance things like a retail center, industrial warehouse, office building and so much more.

A traditional commercial mortgage usually offers a maximum loan amount from 65% to 85% of the loan-to-value ratio of your property. The LTV ratio stands for the fair market value of the property before purchasing it. It means that as a borrower, you should expect to cover from 15% to 35% of the fair market value of the property as the down payment.

With the traditional commercial mortgage, there is no maximum loan amount. The reason is that these mortgages do not have the support or backing of the federal government and thus, the overall loan amounts are up to you, the individual lender.

Where can you get a traditional commercial mortgage? Simple: traditional banks and lending institutions issue traditional commercial mortgages. These mortgages are usually held on the bank's balance sheet as an investment. One example that offers commercial real estate loans on the US Bank.

Angel Investor

Also known as informal investor, business angel, private or seed investor, and sometimes angel funder, an angel investor is a wealthy person who provides capital for a startup, often in exchange for ownership equity or convertible debt.

An angel investor will often put in up to $100,000 and can even take part in priced or debt rounds; however, these individuals tend to be valuation sensitive. You have to be able to distinguish between professional or active and occasional angels.

A good place to start is AngelList, which is a good resource that makes the process of finding angels in your industry or region easier. Check it out to get started. As you look them up on the AngelList, ask how many deals they conduct per year. If an investor only does a couple of deals in a year, talk to such an investor only after he or she approaches you, someone gives you a good introduction, or you are sure the investor has some good experience and background in your space. Otherwise, you should not have infrequent investors on your target list; the occasional angel investors typically take longer to close and tend to be flakier.

A professional or active angel does at least six deals every year. Within the first three meetings, you can expect to close the investor but you can ask if they are interested at the closure of the first meeting, and it is actually a good idea to do so.

NOTE: Before meeting an angel, understand what interests the investor. Do not just approach people randomly. You will only be wasting your time.

The next two options are best suited for someone who already has an established flipping business and with a record of success.

Micro VCs

A VC or venture capital is a newer brand of investor that takes the form of private equity or a type of financing provided by funds or firms. These investors are either people writing $100,000 checks (or more) or firms with about $10 million to $50 million under management. They are like angel investors with more amounts to invest. After two or three meetings, they will say no or commit to invest. They may also lead and be okay with debt or equity.

In New York City, VCs usually invest about $250,000 to $500,000; they can price and lead your round. These investors usually look at ownership but not as much as the typical VC. They will not seek for 20% of your company, but something more like 8 to 10 percent and then increase their investment in the next round—this however depends on the size of their finances.

Just like angels, you will have to determine if a particular micro VC is right for you. Take your time to study their portfolios so that you understand each fund and each partner as that is imperative. Partners usually have different focus areas and experiences, and different preferences for the companies as well. You need to target particular partners at a particular fund.

For a list of active micro VCs, click this link.

Angel Group

As the name implies, an angel group is a group of investors who share a deal flow. These kinds of financiers can conduct priced rounds, and when a good percentage of them are interested, they can quickly lead your deal.

Angel groups have regular meetings as well as regular pitch processes. Some of them conduct more due diligence than the rest but in general, a number of the members of a particular group are usually assigned to do the due diligence when the initial pitch is successful.

What should you expect? Typically, your check may range from $50,000 to $500,000. You have to note that angel groups are not syndicates, and they do not carry fees (unlike AngelList syndicates). The angel groups are also sensitive to valuations, and when you compare them to venture capitalists, you will realize that they price their rounds to a lesser degree.

Look at these angel groups and choose the right one for you to get started.

CONCLUSION

We have come to the end of the book. Thank you for reading and congratulations for reading until the end.

I truly hope that you have found the book eye opening and practical enough for you to start taking immediate action. In fact, at this point, you should be ready to evaluate property and make the right steps to purchase it so that you sell it for profit. The whole process can seem intricate if you are just getting started but with time, you will get used to it and become a pro investor in real estate. As you already have found out, you don't need a lot of money in the bank to invest in real estate as a flipper or a wholesaler; what you need to do is to get out there and:

✓ Meet people especially those who can finance your venture. Networking is a MUST.
✓ Get your hands dirty in finding properties to flip
✓ Know how to do estimates correctly
✓ Get your hands dirty in the process of fixing the property
✓ Get things done from start to finish with lightning speed

As you do everything, don't overlook the importance of professionals, as they will help you to avoid making avoidable mistakes.

If you found the book valuable, can you recommend it to others? One way to do that is to post a review on Amazon.

Click here to leave a review for this book on Amazon!

Thank you and good luck!